Celebrate Recovery

Moving Forward in God's Grace

The Journey Continues

PARTICIPANT'S GUIDE 5

John Baker is the founder of Celebrate Recovery®, a ministry started at Saddleback Church. It is estimated that over the last 25 years more than 1.5 million people have gone through this Christ-centered recovery program. There are currently over 27,000 churches that have weekly Celebrate Recovery meetings.

John has been on staff since Celebrate Recovery started. He has served as the Pastor of Membership, the Pastor of Ministries, and is currently the Pastor of Saddleback Church's Signature Ministries. He is also serving as one of the nine Elder Pastors at Saddleback. John is a nationally known speaker and trainer in helping churches start Celebrate Recovery ministries.

John's writing accomplishments include Celebrate Recovery's *The Journey Begins* Curriculum, *Life's Healing Choices*, the *Celebrate Recovery Study Bible* (general editor), and *The Landing* and *Celebration Place* (coauthor). John's newest books are *Your First Step to Celebrate Recovery* and *The Celebrate Recovery Devotional* (coauthor).

John and his wife Cheryl, the cofounder of Celebrate Recovery, have been married for more than four decades and have served together in Celebrate Recovery since the beginning. They have two adult children, Laura and Johnny, and five grandchildren.

Johnny Baker has been on staff at Celebrate Recovery since 2004 and has been the Pastor of Celebrate Recovery at Saddleback Church since 2012. As an adult child of an alcoholic who chose to become an alcoholic himself, Johnny is passionate about breaking the cycle of dysfunction in his family and helping other families find the tools that will lead to healing and openness. He knows that because of Jesus Christ, and by continuing to stay active in Celebrate Recovery, Maggie, Chloe, and Jimmy—his three children—will never see him drink. Johnny is a nationally recognized speaker, trainer, and teacher of Celebrate Recovery. He is a coauthor of the *Celebrate Recovery Daily Devotional, Celebration Place*, and *The Landing*, and is an associate editor of the *Celebrate Recovery Study Bible*. He has been married since 2000 to his wife Jeni, who serves alongside him in Celebrate Recovery.

Celebrate Recovery®

Moving Forward in God's Grace

PARTICIPANT'S GUIDE 5

The Journey Continues

A recovery program based on eight principles from the Beatitudes

JOHN BAKER & JOHNNY BAKER

FOREWORD BY RICK WARREN

ZONDERVAN®

ZONDERVAN

Moving Forward in God's Grace

Requests for information should be addressed to:
Zondervan, 3900 *Sparks Dr. SE, Grand Rapids, Michigan 49546*

ISBN 978-0-310-13146-5 (softcover)
ISBN 978-0-310-13147-2 (ebook)

Cover design: Brand Navigation
Cover photography: 123rf.com

First Printing May 2016 / Printed in the United States of America

Contents

Foreword

The best known ministry at Saddleback Church—that is going to last for easily 100, maybe 200 years—started when a guy, who was a drunk, came to me with a 13-page letter. And that ministry is called Celebrate Recovery®.

Now, let me just put this in perspective. This may be Saddleback's greatest contribution to the world. Over 20,000 people have completed the step studies at Saddleback's Celebrate Recovery. Over three and a half million people worldwide have gone through a Celebrate Recovery step study.

Right now, around the world, 27,000 churches are using Saddleback's ministry called Celebrate Recovery—27,000 churches! It is so successful that Celebrate Recovery is the official recovery program in 44 state and federal prison systems. It has been translated into 20 different languages.

Do you think John Baker, when he came to see me in my office many years ago and said, "I've got an idea for a ministry, Pastor Rick," imagined it would be affecting three and a half million people in 27,000 churches? No. You have no idea what God wants to do through you. You may have the next big ministry idea. You may have the next Celebrate Recovery dwelling in you—a ministry that could be started and reproduced to bless the whole world. One guy, out of his own pain, starts a ministry that now affects tens of thousands of churches and millions of people.

Rick Warren

(Excerpted from Pastor Warren's talk at Angel Stadium on Saddleback's 35th anniversary)

Introduction

See, I am doing a new thing! Now it springs up;
do you not perceive it? (Isaiah 43:19)

Welcome to *The Journey Continues*!

We are so excited for you as you continue to grow on the road to recovery! If you are starting *The Journey Continues*, it means a few things about you. First, it means you are ready to take the next step on your recovery journey and take your recovery to the next level. It also means that you have already completed at least one *The Journey Begins* (the original Celebrate Recovery® Participant's Guides 1–4) step study group. Last, it means that you have had some time, probably at least six months since completing that study, to begin applying the Biblical Principles of Recovery to your life.

Here in *The Journey Continues* you will build on what you learned about Christ and yourself in *The Journey Begins*, grow deeper in your faith, and strengthen your recovery. You'll find brand new acrostics, new questions, and of course, hundreds of Bible verses. Just as in *The Journey Begins*, you'll grow closer to Christ and the other members of your group as you dig deeper into your life and find freedom in new areas.

To begin *The Journey Continues,* you will see if DENIAL has snuck back into your life in any way and, if so, what to do about it. Since you learned what you give up when you admitted your powerlessness in *The Journey Begins*, here you will explore what God's POWER can do in your life and will see how keeping your HOPE in God can maintain your SANITY. Because you have already turned your life over to Christ, in or before you completed Principle 3 of *The Journey Begins*, you will focus here on the daily ACTIONS you need to take to turn your WILL to Him.

Make sure you take the time to write out your answers before you meet with your group each week. The more you put in to this study, the more you'll get out of it. We will be praying for you as you continue your recovery journey.

"The Lord makes firm the steps of the one who delights in him; though he may stumble, he will not fall, for the Lord upholds him with his hand" (Psalm 37:23–24).

In His steps,
John Baker
Johnny Baker

The Road to Recovery

Eight Principles Based on the Beatitudes

By Pastor Rick Warren

1. **R**ealize I'm not God. I admit that I am powerless to control my tendency to do the wrong thing and that my life is unmanageable. (Step 1)
   "Happy are those who know that they are spiritually poor."
   (Matthew 5:3)
2. **E**arnestly believe that God exists, that I matter to Him, and that He has the power to help me recover. (Step 2)
   "Happy are those who mourn, for they shall be comforted."
   (Matthew 5:4)
3. **C**onsciously choose to commit all my life and will to Christ's care and control. (Step 3)
   "Happy are the meek." (Matthew 5:5)
4. **O**penly examine and confess my faults to myself, to God, and to someone I trust. (Steps 4 and 5)
   "Happy are the pure in heart." (Matthew 5:8)
5. **V**oluntarily submit to any and all changes God wants to make in my life and humbly ask Him to remove my character defects. (Steps 6 and 7)
   "Happy are those whose greatest desire is to do what God requires." (Matthew 5:6)
6. **E**valuate all my relationships. Offer forgiveness to those who have hurt me and make amends for harm I've done to others when possible, except when to do so would harm them or others. (Steps 8 and 9)
   "Happy are the merciful." (Matthew 5:7)
   "Happy are the peacemakers." (Matthew 5:9)
7. **R**eserve a time with God for self-examination, Bible reading, and prayer in order to know God and His will for my life and to gain the power to follow His will. (Steps 10 and 11)
8. **Y**ield myself to God to be used to bring this Good News to others, both by my example and my words. (Step 12)
   "Happy are those who are persecuted because they do what God requires." (Matthew 5:10)

Twelve Steps and Their Biblical Comparisons*

1. We admitted we were powerless over our addictions and compulsive behaviors, that our lives had become unmanageable. I know that nothing good lives in me, that is, in my sinful nature.

   "For I know that good itself does not dwell in me, that is, in my sinful nature. For I have the desire to do what is good, but I cannot carry it out." (Romans 7:18)

2. We came to believe that a power greater than ourselves could restore us to sanity.

   "For it is God who works in you to will and to act in order to fulfill his good purpose." (Philippians 2:1)

3. We made a decision to turn our lives and our wills over to the care of God.

   "Therefore, I urge you, brothers and sisters, in view of God's mercy, to offer your bodies as a living sacrifice, holy and pleasing to God—this is your true and proper of worship." (Romans 12:1)

4. We made a searching and fearless moral inventory of ourselves.

   "Let us examine our ways and test them, and let us return to the Lord." (Lamentations 3:40)

5. We admitted to God, to ourselves, and to another human being the exact nature of our wrongs.

   "Therefore confess your sins to each other and pray for each other so that you may be healed." (James 5:16)

6. We were entirely ready to have God remove all these defects of character.

   "Humble yourselves before the Lord, and he will lift you up." (James 4:10)

7. We humbly asked Him to remove all our shortcomings.

   "If we confess our sins, he is faithful and will forgive us our sins and purify us from all unrighteousness." (1 John 1:9)

8. We made a list of all persons we had harmed and became willing to make amends to them all.

   "Do to others as you would have them do to you." (Luke 6:31)

9. We made direct amends to such people whenever possible, except when to do so would injure them or others.

   "Therefore, if you are offering your gift at the altar and there remember that your brother or sister has something against you, leave your gift there in front of the altar. First go and be reconciled to them; then come and offer your gift." (Matthew 5:23–24)

10. We continued to take personal inventory and when we were wrong, promptly admitted it.

    "So, if you think you are standing firm, be careful that you don't fall!" (1 Corinthians 10:12)

11. We sought through prayer and meditation to improve our conscious contact with God, praying only for knowledge of His will for us, and power to carry that out.

    "Let the message of Christ dwell among you richly." (Colossians 3:16)

12. Having had a spiritual experience as the result of these steps, we try to carry this message to others and practice these principles in all our affairs.

    "Brothers and sisters, if someone is caught in a sin, you who live by the Spirit should restore that person gently. But watch yourselves, or you also may be tempted." (Galatians 6:1)

* Throughout this material, you will notice several references to the Christ-centered 12 Steps. Our prayer is that Celebrate Recovery will create a bridge to the millions of people who are familiar with the secular 12 Steps (we acknowledge the use of some material from the 12 Suggested Steps of Alcoholics Anonymous) and in so doing, introduce them to the one and only true Higher Power, Jesus Christ. Once they begin that relationship, asking Christ into their hearts as Lord and Savior, true healing and recovery can begin!

Serenity Prayer

God, grant me the serenity
to accept the things I cannot change,
the courage to change the things I can,
and the wisdom to know the difference.
Living one day at a time,
enjoying one moment at a time ;
accepting hardship as a pathway to peace;
taking, as Jesus did,
this sinful world as it is,
not as I would have it;
trusting that You will make all things right
if I surrender to Your will;
so that I may be reasonably happy in this life
and supremely happy with You forever in the next.
Amen.

Reinhold Niebuhr

Celebrate Recovery's Small Group Guidelines

The following five guidelines will ensure that your small group is a safe place. They need to be read at the beginning of every meeting.

1. Keep your sharing focused on your own thoughts and feelings. Limit your sharing to three to five minutes.
2. There is NO cross talk. Cross talk is when two individuals engage in conversation excluding all others. Each person is free to express his or her feelings without interruptions.
3. We are here to support one another, not "fix" another.
4. Anonymity and confidentiality are basic requirements. What is shared in the group stays in the group. The only exception is when someone threatens to injure themselves or others.
5. Offensive language has no place in a Christ-centered recovery group.

Lesson 1

Denial

Principle 1: Realize I'm not God. I admit that I am powerless to control my tendency to do the wrong thing and that my life is unmanageable.

"Happy are those who know they are spiritually poor."
(Matthew 5:3)

Step 1: We admitted we were powerless over our addictions and compulsive behaviors, that our lives had become unmanageable.

"I know that good itself does not dwell in me, that is, in my sinful nature. For I have the desire to do what is good, but I cannot carry it out." (Romans 7:18)

Please begin your time together by reading "The First Step, Day 1" of the *Celebrate Recovery Daily Devotional.*

As we begin *The Journey Continues,* we each need to start off by answering this one question: "Have I put on the mask of denial again"?

Before you can make any further progress in this exciting new step study, you need to face your denial. It doesn't matter how long you have been in recovery—you may have been working the steps and principles for years—denial can rear its ugly head and return at any time! You may trade addictions, begin new compulsive behaviors, or be on the road to relapse without even knowing it. By removing your mask of denial, you can take your recovery to the next level, or your recovery can even begin again! Even if you feel that you haven't actively stepped back into denial, denial is something you must be on guard against.

We need to begin *The Journey Continues* by searching our hearts to see if we have allowed any denial back into our recovery. So let's get this new exciting journey started!

DENIAL

D—Disrupts our progress in our recoveries

Hiding our feelings, returning to denial, freezes our recovery and binds our progress.

"Be diligent in these matters; give yourself wholly to them, so that everyone may see your progress." (1 Timothy 4:15)

"Would not God have discovered it, since he knows the secrets of the heart?" (Psalm 44:21)

E—Enables old hurts, hang-ups, and habits to return

As we continue to go through this program, we learn that it is only in the present that positive change can occur. The return of old hurts, hang-ups, and habits makes us unable to live and enjoy God's plans for us in the present.

"As a dog returns to its vomit, so fools repeat their folly." (Proverbs 26:11)

N—Negatively affects the repair work we have done on our relationships

As we slip back into denial, we again start to isolate from those close to us. We start to destroy the new trust and fellowship we have been given by them.

"My friends and companions avoid me because of my wounds; my neighbors stay far away." (Psalm 38:11)

"All this I saw, as I applied my mind to everything done under the sun. There is a time when a man lords it over others to his own hurt." (Ecclesiastes 8:9)

> *The guilty man is the one who wants to be alone; the man who is right with God does not. . . . The final curse of a disobedient soul is that it becomes a separate, self-conscious individual.*
>
> —Oswald Chambers

I—Interrupts our daily walk with God

As we slip further into our denial, it is harder for us to maintain our closeness to God. We think we are fooling everyone, even God. But we are only fooling ourselves.

"Anyone who runs ahead and does not continue in the teaching of Christ does not have God; whoever continues in the teaching has both the Father and the Son." (2 John 1:9)

"Whoever is not with me is against me, and whoever does not gather with me scatters." (Luke 11:23)

A—Allows risk of possible relapse

As we decrease our closeness to God and others, the more we increase the chance of relapse.

"This is what the LORD says: Stand at the crossroads and look; ask for the ancient paths, ask where the good way is, and walk in it, and you will find rest for your souls. But you said, 'We will not walk in it.'" (Jeremiah 6:16)

L—Loss of valuable time

The longer we keep our denial hidden, the more time we are wasting that could be spent on continuing to grow. We need to ask God to help us break free from our denial and continue our forward journey in recovery.

"Therefore, since we are surrounded by such a great cloud of witnesses, let us throw off everything that hinders and the sin that so easily entangles. And let us run with perseverance the race marked out for us." (Hebrews 12:1)

"If anyone, then, knows the good they ought to do and doesn't do it, it is sin for them." (James 4:17)

> *The greatest wasteland in all of our earth ... our waste of the time that God has given us each day.*
>
> —Billy Graham

Questions for Reflection and Discussion

1. Have you noticed that your recovery has been stalled? In what ways has your joy and serenity faded? Describe in detail.

2. Have you begun to believe that you have control over certain aspects of your life? If so, which ones?

3. Have any of your old hurts, hang-ups, or habits begun to fill your mind? (Ask your sponsor or accountability partners if they have seen any old or new negative patterns emerging in you.)

4. Have you begun to struggle with or lost any of your important relationships? List each of them and describe the struggle.

5. In the last six months, have you grown closer to or farther away from God? Describe why you think it has changed.

6. As completely as you can, describe your relationship with God today.

7. Have you been having any thoughts of "the good old days"? Any thoughts that you can handle your struggles differently this time? Write down the specific thoughts you been having.

8. List some of the tools that help you from slipping back into denial. Are you using them?

9. How do you continue to use your time to help newcomers? How do you help ensure others that they are not stuck in denial? (Be specific; everyone in your group will benefit from your answers.)

Prayer

God, thank You for this time together. Thank You for everyone here today. Lord, we ask You to examine our hearts to see if we have allowed any denial back into our recoveries. If we have and we can't see it, open our eyes so we can expose it to Your light.

As we join together, as our journey continues, help us grow closer to You and to one another. It is in Your Son's precious name we pray. Amen.

Lesson 2

Power

Principle 1: Realize I'm not God. I admit that I am powerless to control my tendency to do the wrong thing and that my life is unmanageable.

"Happy are those who know they are spiritually poor." (Matthew 5:3)

Step 1: We admitted we were powerless over our addictions and compulsive behaviors, that our lives had become unmanageable.

"I know that good itself does not dwell in me, that is, in my sinful nature. For I have the desire to do what is good, but I cannot carry it out." (Romans 7:18)

Please begin your time together by reading "Casting Anxiety, Day 12" from the *Celebrate Recovery Daily Devotional.*

In Lesson 2 of *The Journey Begins,* we looked at the "serenity robbers" we would give up when we admitted we were powerless. By admitting our powerlessness, we find that there is a true Higher Power, whose name is Jesus, who can and will restore us to sanity. And He can do so much more!

You are either going to serve God or self. You can't do both! Matthew 6:24 (GNT) says, "No one can be a slave to two masters; he will hate one and love the other; he will be loyal to one and despise the other." Another term for serving "ourselves" is serving the "flesh." *Flesh* is the Bible's word for our unperfected human nature, our sin nature.

If you leave the "h" off the end of *flesh* and reverse the remaining letters, you spell the word *self*. Flesh is the self-life. It is what we are when we are left to our own devices. When our "self" is out of control, all attempts at control—of self or others—fail. In fact, our attempt to control ourselves and others is what got us into trouble in the first place. To have long-lasting peace in your life, God needs to be the one in control.

Because you now have a relationship with Jesus, you now have the POWER to overcome any hurt, hang-up, or habit. Let's look at what that power can do in your life.

POWER

P—Peace of mind can be found

Instead of having our minds racing, trying to keep all of the plates spinning, we can now enjoy the peace of mind that God offers. Then we can turn from trying to do things on our own power and rely on His instead.

And the peace of God, which transcends all understanding, will guard your hearts and your minds in Christ Jesus. (Philippians 4:7)

"Now may the Lord of peace himself give you peace at all times and in every way. The Lord be with all of you." (2 Thessalonians 3:16)

O—Overcoming temptation is possible

Once it may have felt that temptation was impossible to resist. Now that we have God's power, we have the ability to look for ways to escape temptation before giving in.

"No temptation has overtaken you except what is common to mankind. And God is faithful; he will not let you be tempted beyond what you can bear. But when you are tempted, he will also provide a way out so that you can endure it." (1 Corinthians 10:13)

"So I say, walk by the Spirit, and you will not gratify the desires of the flesh." (Galatians 5:16)

W—Worrying can stop

Worry happens when we face a problem bigger than ourselves. When we know that we can't solve a problem with our own power, or when we fear that we will be overcome by something we can't handle, we worry. However, when we trust God and plug into His power through prayer, we find we can stop worrying because nothing is too big for God to handle.

"Therefore do not worry about tomorrow, for tomorrow will worry about itself. Each day has enough trouble of its own." (Matthew 6:34)

"Those who know your name trust in you, for you, LORD, have never forsaken those who seek you." (Psalm 9:10)

E—Every character defect can be healed

There's no issue that God can't heal. Even after completing a step study, we may be holding onto things we have been unwilling to face. We may have some hurts we are afraid to hand over to God, or a secondary recovery issue that we have not dealt with. We now have the power to face them because of God's power. There isn't a character defect or issue in the world that God can't heal!

"He heals the brokenhearted and binds up their wounds." (Psalm 147:3)

R—Real relationships can be formed

Denial and the refusal to admit we have had problems caused us to lose or damage many of our relationships in the past. Coming out of denial, and admitting we are powerless, gives us the ability to stop trying to act like we have it all together and form true trust and intimacy with others.

"For just as each of us has one body with many members, and these members do not all have the same function, so in Christ we, though many, form one body, and each member belongs to all the others." (Romans 12:4–6)

"And let us consider how we may spur one another on toward love and good deeds, not giving up meeting together, as some are in the habit of doing, but encouraging one another—and all the more as you see the Day approaching." (Hebrews 10:24–25)

Questions for Reflection and Discussion

1. Have you fully admitted your powerlessness over your life's hurts, hang-ups, and habits? If not, what's holding you back?

2. How have you experienced "the peace of God, which transcends all understanding"? Share details.

3. How are you plugging into God's power when you are stressed?

4. Share a time when you have felt God's power help you overcome a temptation. Be specific.

5. Sharing a victory over temptation with a newcomer is so important! Who do you know that would be encouraged by hearing that story?

6. What are you worried about today? How can you turn that worry over to God?

7. Now that you've been in recovery for a while, what character defects are you planning on focusing on during *The Journey Continues*?

8. Have you been holding back a particular hurt, hang-up, or habit that you are now ready to face? If so, what is it?

9. Question 6 of the POWERLESS lesson in Participant's Guide 1, *The Journey Begins* asks, "How has your denial isolated you from your important relationships?" Have you seen any change in those relationships since your involvement in Celebrate Recovery? If so, what has happened? If not, why not?

10. What healthy, real relationships have you formed in Celebrate Recovery, and how have they helped your recovery journey?

Prayer

Dear God, please continue to give me the power to overcome my hurts, hang-ups, and habits. I know I need to stop pretending I have it all under control, and that I need to rely on Your power. Help me overcome temptations and worry, and allow me to lean on the people You have placed in my life. Amen.

Lesson 3

HOPE

Principle 2: Earnestly believe that God exists, that I matter to Him, and that He has the power to help me recover.

"Happy are those who mourn, for they shall be comforted." (Matthew 5:4)

Step 2: We came to believe that a power greater than ourselves could restore us to sanity.

"For it is God who works in you to will and to act in order to fulfill his good purpose." (Philippians 2:13)

Please begin your time together by reading "The Second Step, Day 30" from the *Celebrate Recovery Daily Devotional.*

In the *The Journey Begins* step study, we learned that HOPE is being open to change. However, some of us were afraid to change, even if our past was very painful. We resisted change because of our fear of the unknown, or, in our despair, we thought we didn't deserve anything better.

Here's the good news: Hope opens doors where despair closes them! Hope discovers what *can* be done instead of grumbling about what *can't* be done.

We understand throughout our lives that we will continue to encounter hurts and trials that we are powerless to change, but with God's help, we can be open to allow those circumstances and situations to change us—to make us better, not bitter.

Ephesians 4:23 gives us a challenge to that end: "Be made new in the attitude of your minds."

However, as the months and years have passed since your last step study, you might have slowly confused or forgotten where your true, lasting Hope comes from. Sadly, the farther we get from the early days of our recovery, the more we can begin to forget or minimize the people and tools that allowed us to get where we are today. One of the major things we can minimize is just how important our total surrender to God was and is.

HOPE

H—Hope comes from God

We cannot have continued healing from our hurts, hang-ups, and habits without hope. Real hope can only come from God. If we place our hope in people or things, we will come up empty. But when we trust in God, our hope is secure.

"Hopes placed in mortals die with them; all the promise of their power comes to nothing." (Proverbs 11:7)

"Yes, my soul, find rest in God; my hope comes from him." (Psalm 62:5)

"May the God of hope fill you with all joy and peace as you trust in him, so that you may overflow with hope by the power of the Holy Spirit." (Romans 15:13)

O—Open our hearts to allow God to restore all our hope in Him

If we are feeling hopeless, it may be that we have closed our hearts to God. God will not force His love or hope on us. In order for hope to be restored in our lives, we need to open ourselves and invite Him to work in us.

"Why, my soul, are you downcast? Why so disturbed within me? Put your hope in God, for I will yet praise him, my Savior and my God." (Psalm 42:5)

"When anxiety was great within me, your consolation brought me joy." (Psalm 94:19)

P—Purpose for our life is found in Christ's hope

When we discover our purpose, serving God and others, we are filled with hope!

"However, as it is written: 'What no eye has seen, what no ear has heard, and what no human mind has conceived—the things God has prepared for those who love him.'" (1 Corinthians 2:9)

"But I have raised you up for this very purpose, that I might show you my power and that my name might be proclaimed in all the earth." (Exodus 9:16)

> *Everywhere I go I find that people ... both leaders and individuals ... are asking one basic question, "Is there any hope for the future?" My answer is the same, "Yes, through Jesus Christ.*
>
> —Billy Graham

E—Expect and hope for continued new growth and victories!

This study is called *The Journey Continues* for a reason—God isn't finished with us yet. We have more change and victory to come!

"Be joyful in hope, patient in affliction, faithful in prayer." (Romans 12:12)

"Now faith is confidence in what we hope for and assurance about what we do not see." (Hebrews 11:1)

Questions for Reflection and Discussion

1. Today, where is your hope found: in Christ or in someone or something of this world? Why?

2. Summarize just how hopeful in Christ you felt in those early days of recovery. Then write a brief paragraph on how that has changed today. (Has it grown or declined? Why?)

3. What is something that you are discouraged about today? Be specific.

4. Is there anything that you are doubting about your relationship with God today? Again, be specific.

5. What have you discovered as God's purpose for your life?

6. How are you doing at living out that purpose you described in question 5? And with whom have you shared your purpose: someone who could encourage and be objective with you?

7. What are some of the victories you have celebrated by not losing hope?

8. Describe your last experience of sharing the hope found in Christ with a newcomer. (Be specific; everyone in your group will benefit from your answer.)

Prayer

*God, Your Word says, "I pray that God, the source of hope, will fill you completely with joy and peace because you trust in him. Then you will overflow with confident hope through the power of the Holy Spirit."**

God, You are our hope, and that hope is given to us through Your unconditional love for each of us. We pray that we never take it for granted. Help us to share it with others, especially newcomers. Please, God, help us to do this in every opportunity we are given. Amen.

* Romans 15:13, NLT

Lesson 4

SANITY

Principle 2: Earnestly believe that God exists, that I matter to Him, and that He has the power to help me recover.

"Happy are those who mourn, for they shall be comforted." (Matthew 5:4)

Step 2: We came to believe that a power greater than ourselves could restore us to sanity.

"For it is God who works in you to will and to act in order to fulfill his good purpose." (Philippians 2:13)

Please begin your time together by reading "Walk This Way, Day 24" from the *Celebrate Recovery Daily Devotional.*

In Principle 2, we learn how a relationship with Jesus can restore us to SANITY. We defined *sanity* in *The Journey Begins* as a wholeness of mind and spirit. As our recovery journeys continue, we will have times and issues that will try to rob us of that sanity. Even though we are changing, the people and situations around us may not be. In fact, the people in our lives may not even be supportive of our changes. No matter what our situation, we can find the wholeness of mind that we are looking for.

Now that we have that hope, and are continuing to be restored, how do we maintain our sanity?

SANITY

S—Steady growth, not perfection, is the goal

One way to lose our sanity is to look for perfection or complete immediate change. It takes time to overcome our hurts, hang-ups, and habits. Instead of looking for perfection, we need to be on the lookout for all of the small ways we or our loved ones have changed.

"Being confident of this, that he who began a good work in you will carry it on to completion until the day of Christ Jesus." (Philippians 1:6)

"Not that I have already obtained all this, or have already arrived at my goal, but I press on to take hold of that for which Christ Jesus took hold of me. Brothers and sisters, I do not consider myself yet to have taken hold of it. But one thing I do: Forgetting what is behind and straining toward what is ahead, I press on toward the goal to win the prize for which God has called me heavenward in Christ Jesus." (Philippians 3:12–14)

> *We all want progress, but if you're on the wrong road, progress means doing an about-turn and walking back to the right road; in that case, the man who turns back soonest is the most progressive.*
>
> —C. S. Lewis

A—Accept the things I cannot change

The Serenity Prayer reminds us to ask God for the "serenity to accept the things I cannot change." It's in this "accepting" that we are able to remind ourselves that there are things we need to do. Then there are things that only God can do. When we allow God to handle the things we cannot change, we will keep our sanity.

"In peace I will lie down and sleep, for you alone, LORD, make me dwell in safety." (Psalm 4:8)

"Even though I walk through the darkest valley, I will fear no evil, for you are with me; your rod and your staff, they comfort me." (Psalm 23:4)

"Cast all your anxiety on him because he cares for you." (1 Peter 5:7)

N—Notice new hurts, hang-ups, and habits, and take action

If we've been in recovery for a while and still feel as if our life is out of control, it may be that we have issues we have not yet dealt with. It might even be a new issue that started after attending Celebrate Recovery. Whether new issues or unresolved ones from an earlier step study, until they are dealt with, they will cause us to spin out of control.

"But you, man of God, flee from all this, and pursue righteousness, godliness, faith, love, endurance and gentleness." (1 Timothy 6:11)

"Then I acknowledged my sin to you and did not cover up my iniquity. I said, 'I will confess my transgressions to the LORD.' And you forgave the guilt of my sin." (Psalm 32:5)

I—Invite others to help us along the way

One of the most powerful tools we can use to protect our recovery and our sanity is other people. We all must invite other people to hold us accountable and keep us on track. These people have the ability to look into our lives and see things we may not notice on our own.

"Two are better than one, because they have a good return for their labor: If either of them falls down, one can help the other up. But pity anyone who falls and has no one to help them up. . . . Though one may be overpowered, two can defend themselves. A cord of three strands is not quickly broken." (Ecclesiastes 4:9–10, 12)

"And let us consider how we may spur one another on toward love and good deeds, not giving up meeting together, as some are in the habit of doing, but encouraging one another—and all the more as you see the Day approaching." (Hebrews 10:24–25)

T—Try to keep short accounts

While healthy people can help keep us on track, unhealthy relationships can derail us. It would be nice to think that we will never again be hurt by others, but it isn't realistic. While we can't control other people and keep them from hurting us, we can control our response. Instead of holding onto grudges or keeping score, we can extend forgiveness, and make amends, quickly.

"'In your anger do not sin': Do not let the sun go down while you are still angry." (Ephesians 4:26)

"Get rid of all bitterness, rage and anger, brawling and slander, along with every form of malice. Be kind and compassionate to one another, forgiving each other, just as in Christ God forgave you." (Ephesians 4:31–32)

Y—Your Higher Power is on your side!

Remember that you are not alone! Not only do you have the other people sitting in this group with you, but you also have the God who created the universe on your side! You are not alone!

"For God did not appoint us to suffer wrath but to receive salvation through our Lord Jesus Christ." (1 Thessalonians 5:9)

"No temptation has overtaken you except what is common to mankind. And God is faithful; he will not let you be tempted beyond what you can bear. But when you are tempted, he will also provide a way out so that you can endure it." (1 Corinthians 10:13)

"For he has rescued us from the dominion of darkness and brought us into the kingdom of the Son he loves, in whom we have redemption, the forgiveness of sins." (Colossians 1:13–14)

Questions for Reflection and Discussion

1. Since first completing *The Journey Begins* step study, how has your life moved from chaos to hope?

2. What are some steady improvements you have seen in your recovery? Be specific. And how can focusing on these improvements help you keep your sanity?

3. What are some things going on, right now, that are out of your control? Again, be specific.

4. How can you give the things you mentioned in question 3 to Christ? (Write down how giving out-of-control situations to Christ helped you in the past.)

5. Have you noticed any new hurts, hang-ups, or habits since you started recovery? Be specific. If so, what action(s) have you taken to deal with them?

6. Who have you invited to help you on your journey?

7. Share about a time you helped someone else when they needed encouragement in their recovery.

8. How can making amends or quickly offering forgiveness help you keep your sanity? List some examples.

9. How does knowing Jesus is on your side help you in your recovery?

Prayer

Dear God, thank You for helping us make decisions based on Your truth. Today, we can live our lives knowing that we can always put our hope in You. When we face a new struggle, we can turn it over to You. When we need to offer our amends to others, we can do so modeling Your love for us. We pray that others will see more of You and less of us as we continue to grow in our journey. In Your Son's precious name we pray, amen.

Lesson 5

WILL

Principle 3: Consciously choose to commit all my life and will to Christ's care and control.

"Happy are the meek." (Matthew 5:5)

Step 3: We made a decision to turn our lives and our wills over to the care of God.

"Therefore, I urge you, brothers and sisters, in view of God's mercy, to offer your bodies as a living sacrifice, holy and pleasing to God—this is your true and proper worship." (Romans 12:1)

Please begin your time together by reading "The Third Step, Day 60" from the *Celebrate Recovery Daily Devotional.*

In *The Journey Begins* step study, Lesson 5's acrostic is TURN. That is the most important decision we will ever make. But after we decide to turn our lives over to Christ as our Higher Power, Lord and Savior, the next step is to understand and follow God's WILL for our lives. That is a daily, sometimes hourly process. Relying solely on our own understanding is what got most of us into recovery in the first place! Many of us tried to fill God's role and came up empty and broken.

> *The greatest barrier to knowing God's will is simply that we want to run our own lives. Our problem is that a battle is going on in our hearts—a battle between our wills and God's will.*
>
> —Billy Graham

After making the decision to ask Jesus into our lives, we must begin to seek His will in all our decisions. We need to get to know and understand Him and what He wants for our lives. Proverbs 3:5–6 says, "Trust in the Lord with all your heart and lean not on your own understanding; in all your ways acknowledge him, and he will make your paths straight."

Our understanding is earthbound. It's human to the core. Limited. Finite. We operate in a dimension totally unlike that of our Lord. He knows no such limitations. We understand now that God sees forever!

Someday, we will see Jesus face-to-face. The fog of interpretation will be lifted, and our understanding will be perfected. Praise God that we do not need a perfect understanding of Him to ask Jesus into our lives as our Lord and Savior! But we *do* need to be continuously growing in Christ thereafter.

"For now we see only a reflection as in a mirror; then we shall see face to face. Now I know in part; then I shall know fully, even as I am fully known" (1 Corinthians 13:12).

WILL

W—Will is to "Consciously choose to commit all my life and will to Christ's care and control." Principle 3

"Blessed are the meek, for they will inherit the earth." (Matthew 5:5)

Will is the second part of Principle 3. We exchange our will for His. This is a choice we make daily—it won't happen on its own.

"So I say, walk by the Spirit, and you will not gratify the desires of the flesh. For the flesh desires what is contrary to the Spirit, and the Spirit what is contrary to the flesh. They are in conflict with each other, so that you are not to do whatever you want." (Galatians 5:16–17)

"Therefore let us move beyond the elementary teachings about Christ and be taken forward to maturity." (Hebrews 6:1)

I—Initial decision to accept Christ as your Lord and Savior is a one-time decision that you made during your (or before you began) *The Journey Begins* step study

"And you also were included in Christ when you heard the message of truth, the gospel of your salvation. When you believed, you were marked in him with a seal, the promised Holy Spirit." (Ephesians 1:13)

"But grow in the grace and knowledge of our Lord and Savior Jesus Christ. To him be glory both now and forever! Amen." (2 Peter 3:18)

L—Look for God's will in all our decisions. No matter how large or small.

Sometimes we believe that God only cares about the big-picture things, but God's will extends to all areas of our lives. We need to seek Him in every decision.

"Do not conform to the pattern of this world, but be transformed by the renewing of your mind. Then you will be able to test and approve what God's will is–his good, pleasing and perfect will." (Romans 12:2)

"He made known to us the mystery of his will according to his good pleasure, which he purposed in Christ." (Ephesians 1:9)

L—Listen and pray for God's will prior to making our decisions. Share them with our accountability team before making any major decisions.

"Instead, you ought to say, 'If it is the Lord's will, we will live and do this or that.' As it is, you boast in your arrogant schemes. All such boasting is evil. If anyone, then, knows the good they ought to do and doesn't do it, it is sin for them." (James 4:15–17)

"A sluggard is wiser in his own eyes than seven people who answer discreetly." (Proverbs 26:16)

Questions for Reflection and Discussion

1. Since making the decision to follow Christ, how are you continuously learning to grow in Christ? Share details.

2. Why is it important to include God in all your big and small decisions? List at least three reasons.

3. How does it feel when you are living in God's purpose, His will, for your life? List at least three benefits.

4. How does it feel when you find yourself out of God's will? Be specific.

5. Write down the names of your "wise counselors" who can help you discern if a decision you are planning to make is God's will or your own.

6. Describe a couple of recent decisions you made where you "consciously chose to commit all your life and will to Christ's care and control." How did they work out?

7. Describe a couple of recent decisions you made where you basically said, "No problem, God, I got this one." How did those work out?

8. Finally, why would you make any decisions without first seeking God's will for your life? Be honest.

Prayer

Thank You, God, for sending us Your precious Son to die on the cross for all our sins. Thank You for giving us the opportunity to ask Him into our lives as our Lord and Savior. We come to You now asking for your power for each of us to seek Your perfect will. We love You and we want to continue to grow in Your purpose and plan for each of us. Amen.

Lesson 6

Action

Principle 3: Consciously choose to commit all my life and will to Christ's care and control.

"Happy are the meek." (Matthew 5:5)

Step 3: We made a decision to turn our lives and our wills over to the care of God.

"Therefore, I urge you, brothers and sisters, in view of God's mercy, to offer your bodies as a living sacrifice, holy and pleasing to God—this is your true and proper of worship." (Romans 12:1)

Please begin your time together by reading "Course Correction, Day 44" from the *Celebrate Recovery Daily Devotional.*

In *The Journey Begins*, ACTION is all about turning out *lives* over to Christ. It is a one-time decision that is life changing. In the last lesson, we saw the importance of daily turning our will over to God. Now we will look at how to take the action of turning our will over to Him.

ACTION

A—Ask for God's will to be done

Trying to do things our way is what got us into recovery in the first place. Now that we've spent some time in Celebrate Recovery, we know how important it is to follow God's will. In order to thrive in recovery, we need to ask for God to reveal His will to us, and that His will would be done, even if it goes against what we would choose. We need to spend time each day in prayer asking God for His will to be done, making sure to listen for His response.

"Father, if you are willing, take this cup from me; yet not my will, but yours be done." (Luke 22:42)

"Your kingdom come, your will be done, on earth as it is in heaven." (Matthew 6:10)

"Now listen, you who say, 'Today or tomorrow we will go to this or that city, spend a year there, carry on business and make money.' Why, you do not even know what will happen tomorrow. What is your life? You are a mist that appears for a little while and then vanishes. Instead, you ought to say, 'If it is the Lord's will, we will live and do this or that.'" (James 4:13–15)

C—Choose to follow His will over our own

Once we know God's will, we will have to choose to follow it. This may take making day-by-day or moment-by-moment decisions. He may lead us to do something we'd rather not, but He can be trusted.

"Trust in the LORD with all your heart and lean not on your own understanding; in all your ways submit to him, and he will make your paths straight." (Proverbs 3:5–6)

"Since, then, you have been raised with Christ, set your hearts on things above, where Christ is, seated at the right hand of God. Set your minds on things above, not on earthly things." (Colossians 3:1–2)

T—Trust that He has a plan for us

God wants to recycle our pain and experiences to help other people! He wants to use us to reach others. We need to daily trust that God has a plan for us. It might not always feel like it, but we can go to God's Word for reminders when we need them.

"For I know the plans I have for you," declares the LORD, "plans to prosper you and not to harm you, plans to give you hope and a future." (Jeremiah 29:11)

"For we are God's handiwork, created in Christ Jesus to do good works, which God prepared in advance for us to do." (Ephesians 2:10)

I—Invest in others by serving

Again, God wants us to serve other people. He wants to turn our pain into purpose. One way for us to know that we are changing is when we take the focus off ourselves and put it on Christ and others. Notice, this is different from the codependent behaviors we may have developed. This time, we aren't serving other people so they'll love us or because we think we have to. Now we *want* to give back to Jesus because He calls us to.

"You, my brothers and sisters, were called to be free. But do not use your freedom to indulge the flesh; rather, serve one another humbly in love." (Galatians 5:13)

"Each of you should use whatever gift you have received to serve others, as faithful stewards of God's grace in its various forms." (1 Peter 4:10)

O—Obey God's Word

When we talk about discerning God's will, finding God's plan for our lives, and learning how to serve others, we find we aren't left on our own. We have been given a way to find out directly from God what His will is for us: the Bible. We need to daily spend time in the Bible reading about what He wants for us. But we have to do more than just read: we have to apply the truth we find there to our lives!

"Do not merely listen to the word, and so deceive yourselves. Do what it says." (James 1:22)

"Never take your word of truth from my mouth, for I have put my hope in your laws. I will always obey your law, for ever and ever. I will walk about in freedom, for I have sought out your precepts." (Psalm 119:43–45)

N—Notice areas to put our recovery into practice

Since we have been in recovery for a while now, we have experienced amazing changes and found some victory over key areas in our lives. Now, we may find that it's time to work on new things that we didn't know about when we started Celebrate Recovery or that have revealed themselves on the journey.

Take action on those new areas. When God reveals them, face them head-on and apply the truth you have learned in Celebrate Recovery to those areas, too. We aren't looking for freedom from just one area but in all areas of our lives!

"The thief comes only to steal and kill and destroy; I have come that they may have life, and have it to the full." (John 10:10)

Questions for Reflection and Discussion

1. In what areas do you need to seek God's will today? Be specific.

2. How do you know if something is God's will or your own?

3. Share about a time when you chose God's will over your own.

4. What do you think is God's plan for your life?

5. How often do you read the Bible? Have you made a daily quiet time a habit? If not, why not?

6. What are some ways that you can act on what you are learning in God's Word?

7. Who are you serving? How can you use what you've been given to bless others?

8. How specifically can you put your recovery into practice this week?

Prayer

Heavenly Father, please give me the power to choose Your will over my own. Please reveal Your will to me every day. Please show me through Your Word, through other people, and by answering my prayers. I ask for Your love and wisdom and guidance. Amen.

Afterword

Now that you have completed all of the lessons in this participant's guide to the best of your ability, congratulations are most definitely in order!

In Principle 1, you again faced your denial and were reminded of what God's power could do in your life.

"For I know that good itself does not dwell in me, that is, in my sinful nature. For I have the desire to do what is good, but I cannot carry it out." (Romans 7:18)

In Principle 2, you saw how keeping your hope in God could help you maintain your sanity and give you freedom in new areas of your life.

"For it is God who works in you to will and to act in order to fulfill his good purpose." (Philippians 2:13)

In Principle 3, you focused on daily turning your will over to God, asking Him to reveal His perfect will for you as well as what actions to take to stay in step with Him.

"Therefore, I urge you, brothers and sisters, in view of God's mercy, to offer your bodies as a living sacrifice, holy and pleasing to God—this is your true and proper worship." (Romans 12:1)

Now as you get ready to move on to Participant's Guide 6, *Asking God to Grow My Character*, you will again take a moral inventory to help you identify any unresolved issues or expose any new issues that may have surfaced since you started Celebrate Recovery. Remember the victory you experienced when you completed an inventory during *The Journey Begins*, and lean on Jesus Christ and the other people He has placed alongside you on the road to recovery.

ALSO AVAILABLE

CELEBRATE RECOVERY 30 ANNIVERSARY

NIV Celebrate Recovery® Study Bible

The *NIV Celebrate Recovery Study Bible* is a powerful and positive ally. This Bible is based on eight recovery principles found in Jesus' Sermon on the Mount and on the underlying Christ-centered twelve steps of the proven Celebrate Recovery program. Now typeset in Zondervan's exclusive Comfort Print® typeface, this Bible and all of its added content lifts you up and shows you how to walk, step by attainable step, on a path of healing and liberty.

Features:

- The full text of the accurate, readable, and clear New International Version (NIV) translation
- Articles explain eight recovery principles and accompanying Christ-centered twelve steps
- 110 lessons unpack eight recovery principles in practical terms

9780310455257

- Recovery stories offer encouragement and hope
- 30 days of recovery-related readings
- Over 50 full-page biblical character studies are tied to stories from real-life people who have found peace and help with their own hurts, hang-ups, and habits
- Book introductions
- Side-column reference system keyed to Celebrate Recovery's eight recovery principles
- Topical index
- Exclusive Zondervan NIV Comfort Print typeface in 9-point print size

Available now at your favorite bookstore.

ZONDERVAN®